Attitude

"*THE LONGER I LIVE, the more I realize the impact of attitude on life. Attitude, to me, is more important than facts.*

It is more important than the past, than education, than money, than circumstances, than failures, than successes, than what other people think or say or do.

It is more important than appearance, giftedness or skill. It will make or break a company...a church...a home.

The remarkable thing is we have a choice every day regarding the attitude we will embrace for that day.

We cannot change our past...we cannot change the fact that people will act a certain way. We cannot change the inevitable.

The only thing we can do is play on the one string we have, and that is our attitude...

I am convinced that life is 10% what happens to me and 90% how I react to it.

And so it is with you...we are in charge of our attitudes."

By Charles Swindoll

Two Lessons from Pain

BOTH OF US HAVE HAD our share of successes and failures the same as Bill Cosby. Winning was fun. The failures were not. They caused us pain. We learned two valuable lessons from that pain. The first lesson is . . .

☞ **It always takes longer than expected to reach a goal.**

For example, this book took over three years to complete. We never imagined it would take that long. So be prepared to persevere long enough until you succeed. If, after all your efforts don't work, move forward with a lesson learned never to repeat again.

The second lesson was a surprise. At the time of failure it doesn't seem possible that anything positive can happen. But over the years, and only in looking back, have we learned from our pain that . . .

☞ **Something good comes from every failure.**

NOTHING IS AS PAINFUL AS THE LOSS OF UNFULFILLED DREAMS. — Donny and Linkie

The Concept of Achievement

THE ENTIRE CONCEPT of achievement is based on setting goals. When you set goals for yourself, you become a more spirited, enthusiastic and focused individual. Life is more fun.

Most of us fail more often than we succeed. Abraham Lincoln was a prime example. He failed twelve times over twenty-nine years before he was elected president.

Accept the fact that it's not so dreadful to fail. You won't have to disappear off the face of the earth if you make a mistake. We bet your friends won't desert you, neither will your family, and neither will we. But think of the other side of the coin. What if you set a goal and you succeed? What could be more fulfilling and exciting?

Donny and Linkie readily admit they are not perfect.

We certainly don't expect you to be perfect, so please don't try. All of us are only human. Humans weren't created to be perfect.

YOU WERE BORN TO GROW, TO LEARN, TO CREATE, EXPERIENCE LOVE AND JOY, AND SHARE YOUR UNIQUE TALENTS WITH THE WORLD.
— Donny and Linkie

EXPERIMENT #5
ACTION PLAN

AT THE END OF Chapter 2, you rated your Core Values. From your final list of five, decide which one you want to choose for a *Target Goal*. Be sure you feel totally committed to whichever you choose. Know that your heart, and not your head, is directing you to this one goal. Next . . .

ACTION PLAN

1. Target Goal

2. Deadline

3. Supporting Steps

4. My Daily List

1. WRITE YOUR GOAL DOWN

Fill in the Action Plan on the next page.

2. SET A DATE FOR THE ACCOMPLISHMENT

Select the date that you want to complete your goal. Don't rush yourself. There's no need to pressure yourself any more than you are right now. Remember, be kind to yourself. You deserve it.

3. SUPPORTING STEPS

List all the steps you can think of that will support and help you reach your *Target Goal.* To review *Supporting Steps* turn back to page 36 in Chapter 2.

4. MY DAILY LIST

Fill in "My Daily List" on the next page. Divide the list of things you want to do between daytime and evening hours. In the lower right-hand box, write your name in the blank space following, "Something that gives me, (*your name*), satisfaction."

Think about what simple, everyday pleasures give you satisfaction and include them here. Maybe being with friends, or playing with your pet gives you pleasure. Or perhaps making good grades or doing something nice for someone else gives you a lot of enjoyment. The idea is to get used to thinking about and doing things that make you feel good about you.

In the lower left-hand corner, write a commitment to yourself. Example, *"I promise to work toward my Target Goal each day."* Then do what it takes to keep from disappointing yourself.

ACTION PLAN

Name: _____ Today's Date: _____

Target Goal: _____

Date to be completed: _____

My Daily List

Supporting Steps/Daytime	Supporting Steps/Evening
_____	_____
_____	_____
_____	_____
_____	_____
_____	_____
_____	_____
_____	_____

My commitment to me:	Something that gives me,
	_____,
	(name)
	satisfaction:
_____	_____
_____	_____
_____	_____

EXPERIMENT #6
AFFIRMATIONS

★ I am becoming a winner now!

★ I am visualizing my Target Goal now!

★ I am persevering until I accomplish my goal

of _____

_____now!

(fill in this blank)

Close Your Mouth

NOW THAT YOU HAVE COMPLETED these two pages, don't tell a soul. There is a power within you that will cooperate and help you achieve your goals if you will just keep it to yourself. Start learning to trust yourself, to have faith in yourself and your personal power. You really can do it. We know you can.

A VISION WITHOUT PREPARATION, PLANNING AND PERFORMANCE IS JUST ANOTHER DAYDREAM.
— Donny & Linkie

NOTES TO MYSELF

4 Achieving Goals

The Secret to Belonging

> *A GOAL IS A DREAM WITH A DEADLINE.*
> — Donny & Linkie

The Unique You

ARE YOU AWARE OF HOW precious you are? Yes, we mean you! You are not only a special individual, but you were born a *winner*. You are unique and different from every other person in the entire world and here's the proof:

☞ Your physical structure, your facial features, even your hair is different from any one you know, right?

☞ No one else has your set of fingerprints. The police, F.B.I., and other government agencies use fingerprints for identifying individuals suspected of crimes.

☞ Scientists have discovered another method for identifying individuals, called DNA profiling. DNA stands for deoxyribonucleic acid, and is found in blood, bone, hair and semen.

☞ No one else has the same vocal tonality that you have. In fact, you may be identifying yourself through your voice rather than a driver's license in the near future.

☞ For you to have been born, you had to battle fifty million other sperm who were fighting to be born at the same time as you. *You* conquered every obstacle. *You* persevered. ***You won out!***

So what does all of this prove? First, it proves that you began life as a *winner*. So why would you want to be anything other than a *winner*? Secondly, you have the potential to offer something original to contribute to the world that no one else can.

I began a WINNER.
I am still a WINNER!

Check out Your Success Factor

SURELY BY NOW YOU KNOW how we feel about you. Take this opportunity to find out how you feel about yourself. It is all about self-esteem.

How high or low is your self-esteem, your feeling of self-worth? No one else can answer that. It is your call.

You can decide that you are a valuable, respectable, lovable, competent, worthwhile and important human being who agrees with us, or you can decide the exact opposite — all negative traits and qualities not worth putting on this paper.

If you are interested in finding out how you actually feel about yourself, answer the following questions. Give serious thought to each one before checking "yes" or "no."

Self-Esteem Questionnaire

<u>**Yes**</u> <u>**No**</u> <u>**Do You Consider Yourself to Be:**</u>

___ ___ 1. Fun to be with?

___ ___ 2. A good friend?

___ ___ 3. Smart?

___ ___ 4. Level headed?

___ ___ 5. A positive role-model?

___ ___ 6. Attractive?

___ ___ 7. Worthwhile?

___ ___ 8. Acceptable to others?

___ ___ 9. Generous?

___ ___ 10. Tolerant of others not like you?

___ ___ 11. Trustworthy?

___ ___ 12. Able to trust others?

___ ___ 13. Honest about your feelings?

___ ___ 14. Able to share your feelings?

___ ___ 15. Dependable?

___ ___ 16. Willing to learn from your mistakes?

___ ___ 17. Able to accept criticism comfortably?

___ ___ 18. Flexible — willing to change?

___ ___ 19. Developing your talents?

___ ___ 20. Happy for others when they succeed?

___ ___ 21. Able to accept your shortcomings?

___ ___ 22. Loyal?

Yes	No	**Do You Consider Yourself to Be:**
___	___	23. Self disciplined?
___	___	24. Goal oriented?
___	___	25. Able to give love?
___	___	26. Accountable for your actions?
___	___	27. Kind?

Yes	No	**Is It Easy for You To:**
___	___	28. Make new friends?
___	___	29. Accept your love?
___	___	30. Praise others?
___	___	31. Praise yourself?
___	___	32. Laugh at yourself?
___	___	33. Say, *"No!"* to peers when your gut says to?
___	___	34. Admit to making a mistake?
___	___	35. Develop your strengths?
___	___	36. Be friends with those not like you?

Yes	No	**Do You:**
___	___	37. Like yourself?
___	___	38. Trust yourself?
___	___	39. Respect who you are?
___	___	40. Feel confident about your abilities?
___	___	41. Give yourself credit when you deserve it?

<u>Yes</u> <u>No</u>   <u>Do You:</u>

____   ____   42. Encourage yourself to be your best?

____   ____   43. Encourage others to be their best?

____   ____   44. Feel a sense of responsibility to others?

____   ____   45. Have a sense of humor?

____   ____   46. Take on new challenges?

____   ____   47. Avoid pushing people around?

____   ____   48. Take pride in your achievements?

____   ____   49. Accept responsibility for what you do?

____   ____   50. Have high energy and drive?

____   ____   51. Care about others?

____   ____   52. Work to improve yourself?

____   ____   53. Value your closest relationships?

____   ____   54. Express your appreciation to them?

____   ____   55. Feel great about yourself?

___   **TOTAL** of "Yes" answers only

<u>How Did You Do?</u>

TOTAL YOUR "YES" ANSWERS. If you answered all 55 questions "Yes," your self-esteem is abundantly healthy. There is no need for us to applaud you. You're confident enough not to need outside praise.

Here is a challenge. Each "No" answer is worthy of becoming one of your goals — to turn into a "Yes." Choose one "No" and take as much time as you need to turn it into a "Yes."

Continue until you have all 55 "Yes" answers. Don't give up. Persevere. Owning high self-esteem is critical to your future success and to your becoming a *Winner for Life.*

We would guess that most of you reading this didn't reach that magic number of 55 "Yes" answers. If you had asked either of us to answer these same questions at your age, we can assure you we wouldn't have reached 55 "Yes" answers either. Just don't be discouraged. There is hope.

Do You Know of Dr. Wayne Dyer?

MOST PSYCHOLOGISTS AND psychiatrists agree that it is possible to change how you feel about yourself. Dr. Wayne Dyer, famed psychologist and author states,

> *"I believe almost all human problems stem from low self-esteem, from not liking themselves very much. Fears of failure, poverty, rejection, criticism, loss are all a result of low self-esteem. When you genuinely like and respect yourself as a valuable and worthwhile person, the less you fear failure, because you realize your failures are not you. The less you fear rejection, the less you are concerned with what people like or dislike about you, and the more willing you are to reach out to fulfilling your full potential."*

Realize that you can become a person with high self-esteem. You can *make* it happen by being active, creative and mentally tough. Remember, you are becoming what you think about every minute of the day. Focus on your desires. Focus on your *Target Goals.* <u>Act</u> to make them come true.

Could You Give One Hundred Dollars Away?

OWNING HIGH SELF-ESTEEM allows you to like yourself. Eventually you even will be able to love yourself. When you love yourself, you can be more caring, kinder and respectful to others. You are probably wondering what we mean.

Think about it this way. If you wanted to give your best friend a ticket to a concert, or a compact disc, or hundred dollars, those things would have to belong to you. You would have to own them before you could give them away. Right? But then you most likely would want to keep the hundred dollars, so use your imagination for this one.

The same applies to love. If you don't love yourself first, then how can you give your love away to someone else? On that same note, how can you have good feelings about people if you don't own good feelings toward yourself first?

Love Yourself

WHEN YOU LOVE YOURSELF, IT'S EASIER TO FEEL YOU DESERVE TO BE A WINNER IN LIFE. — Donny & Linkie

Know Someone Who Boasts Too Much?

PLEASE UNDERSTAND. When we talk about loving yourself, we are not talking about being cocky or conceited. You know lots of people like that we're sure. They probably have a poor self-image and low self-esteem. They try to cover it up by going to the opposite extreme of bragging and boasting.

There is another kind of person you know as well. We are referring to the person who puts you down or criticizes you. They try to humiliate you, embarrass you and make you feel bad about yourself.

This is just another example of a person with low self-esteem. When they are putting you <u>down</u>, they feel <u>up</u>. It's their way of making themselves feel important. It's also their way of getting attention. These are usually unsuccessful people who, when they are not thinking about themselves, are thinking about lack, loss, limitation and how much everything costs.

What's Showing When You Apply for a Job?

WHEN YOU GET READY to go into the marketplace to apply for a job, realize your self-esteem will be showing. How you feel about yourself will be reflected in the way you walk, the way you talk, the way you sit or stand. Every move you make will tell the other person what you think of yourself. When you have high self-esteem, you can almost touch it. If you have low self-esteem, it is evident as well.

High self-esteem has recently been added to the list of qualities that companies want and expect their employees to have.

Employers today consider it a basic skill that is just as important as reading, writing and math. Three other qualifications employers look for are:

1. Attitude: They want someone who is enthusiastic, easy to get along with, willing to learn and work hard.

2. Education: They prefer a college graduate, but a high school diploma is a must.

3. Experience: Employers want someone who is industrious; who has worked somewhere before they come to apply to them.

A Critical Time for Choices

WE ARE STRESSING the importance of feeling good about yourself because we want you to have all the tools you need to accomplish your *Target Goals* now!

This is a critical stage in your life. Deciding to graduate from high school and hopefully college are two of the most important decisions you will make. That is why we chose to write this book for your particular age group.

We want to think that this book will help you make the right choices not only for your future, but also for the future of our country. Don't forget, you are our future leaders. You are needed!

> **THE REST OF YOUR LIFE DEPENDS ON CHOICES YOU MAKE NOW.** —Donny & Linkie

Have Fun Choosing a Mentor

TO BE A **WINNER**, it is important to study success. Think of all the people you know. Which of them do you consider to be *winners?* Who would you most want to choose as a role model? Take time to consider that question. Once you make that decision, ask that person to be your mentor.

A mentor is a "wise advisor, a teacher, a friend, a coach." Wouldn't you like to have someone like that in your life? You can. All you have to do is <u>ask</u>.

This person might be a religious leader, a business person, someone important in your community, an older brother or sister, a grandparent, a teacher, or maybe one of your parents or adopted parents.

In our experience, we have found that the more successful people are, the nicer they are. Why? Because they own high self-esteem! They don't feel threatened by anyone, and therefore it is easier for them to be nice to everyone.

It would be wise to choose someone whose career matches your interests. Meet with them on a regular basis. Listen to them. Study them. Ask them to tell you their story.

Ask about their failures as well as their successes. Together, strategize your future. Learn everything you can from them.

Here Is a Warning

BE PREPARED FOR rejection. The person you ask may refuse your request. Why? Because they are *winners* and *winners* are constantly striving for higher goals as well as helping others. They may not have enough time for you right now. Just don't take it personally.

Be bold; be courageous. Keep asking. Even if it takes five, six or even ten tries before you get a *"yes."* Don't give up. Persevere. Even if you don't feel like a *winner* to start with, if you will <u>act</u> like a *winner*, do the same things that other *winners* do, you eventually will begin to feel self-confident, competent and unafraid of anything. You might want to check out Experiment #7 at the end of this chapter before you ask someone to be your mentor.

> *"NEVER GIVE IN. NEVER GIVE IN. NEVER. NEVER. NEVER. NEVER IN ANYTHING GREAT OR SMALL, LARGE OR PETTY; NEVER GIVE IN EXCEPT TO CONVICTIONS OF HONOR AND GOOD SENSE."*
> — **Winston Churchill**
> **Prime Minister, England**

The Woman Who Gave Up Too Soon

THIS STORY IS ABOUT a woman who would never give in. Her name is Florence Chadwick. At twenty-four years of age she was a world-renowned long distance swimmer. Florence broke all existing records for swimming the English Channel from both directions. In the summer of 1952, she decided to swim twenty-two miles of the Catalina Channel in California.

The day of the event the area was blanketed by fog. As millions of people watched from the shoreline and on their television sets, Florence waded into the water. Hour after hour ticked off as she fought bone-chilling cold, fog and shark infested waters. Several times sharks had to be driven away with rifle shots to keep her from being eaten alive.

She became desperate as she tried to make out the shoreline through her swimmer's goggles. After fifteen hours and fifty-five minutes, frozen to the bone, she asked to be pulled into the boat. Once ashore Chadwick was heartbroken to learn she was only one-half mile from her **Target Goal.** She told the news reporters, "*If I could have seen land, I know I could have made it.*"

Determined not to quit a loser, two months later she swam the same channel blanketed by fog, as before. Only this time she made it.

Are you wondering what changed? It was her *Winning-Edge Attitude.* She didn't let the fog defeat her. Chadwick swam with the picture of land firmly entrenched in her mind, and the faith in her heart that she could make it to shore.

Not only was Florence Chadwick the first woman to swim the Catalina Channel, she also beat the men's record by two hours!

Worth Repeating!

PLEASE GIVE YOURSELF the best chance you can in life. Believe in yourself. Let your dreams, desires, visions, goals become a reality. Be all that you can be. If a goal has come into your mind, you are bound to have the ability necessary to accomplish it.

Be accountable to yourself. Once you make a decision to do something, don't disappoint yourself. Upon accomplishment, reward yourself. Be kind to yourself, you deserve it. Life is not a constant win or lose battle. It is full of challenges and opportunities.

YOU ARE AN IMPORTANT PART OF THIS UNIVERSE. WITHOUT YOU, THERE WOULD BE AN IRREPLACEABLE VOID. — Donny & Linkie

EXPERIMENT #7
ACTION STEP

THIS ACTION STEP IS going to be a game — one you play by yourself, against yourself. Go back to the Self-Esteem Questionnaire and read number 30. Do you know how to praise others? Do you ever do it? Since we know few adults who praise others, you probably never had anyone to copy. To play the game follow the instructions below:

1. Select seven people you like a lot. Try including one or two adults.

2. Write their names in the "Self-Esteem Game" form on page 79.

3. Decide whether each one has "high" or "low," self-esteem. Mark your answer under "Your Guess."

4. Next, praise each of the seven. Be sure the two of you are alone at the time you are ready to praise them.

I have HIGH self-esteem.

I want you to have high self-esteem too!

EXPERIMENT #7
ACTION STEP

5. After you have given your praise, stand still with your eyes wide open and examine their reaction. <u>The first thirty seconds is critical</u>. Watch carefully their facial and body reactions. If they look at you as if they don't believe you, you will know that they probably have "low" self-esteem. If they start laughing, or make fun of you, or say something like, '*You've got to be kidding,*" can you guess where their self-esteem is? Wouldn't you guess "low?" We would.

   However, if they accept your words easily, smile and even say "*Thank you,*" you know that person surely has a sense of "high" self-esteem.

6. To score, match your first answer with the one you chose after you praised them Count how many you got right. <u>To win the game you have to guess all seven correctly.</u>

The key to this game will be your sincerity. Avoid complementing/praising/validating your friends about their looks or their clothes. You can use the Self-Esteem Game to pick out qualities that fit them if you can't think of anything else to say. We promise if you are serious and sincere when you validate your seven, they will have to believe what you are saying about them.

We hope you will keep playing this game until you do get seven correct answers. Then keep validating people. Seek out someone each day of the week. Make it a habit. If you want to feel like you "belong" this is one sure way to get there.

THE SELF-ESTEEM GAME

NAME	YOUR GUESS: HIGH	LOW	ACTUAL RESULT: HIGH	LOW
1.				
2.				
3.				
4.				
5.				
6.				
7.				

After you have completed this game take stock of yourself. See if you feel any differently about yourself than you did before you started. Our guess is that you will feel better about yourself. Why? First, because you chose a goal and completed it; second, because you helped someone else feel good about themselves. That will surely make you feel good about yourself.

Start praising others regularly. It is another way to increase your self-esteem. By the way, when you find someone with high self-esteem, you may want to be around that person as often as possible.

EXPERIMENT #8

AFFIRMATIONS

BEGIN SAYING THESE Affirmations in the morning when you are brushing your teeth and looking into the mirror. Take forty-two seconds longer to look at yourself — we mean *really* look at yourself. Who do you see? Is it someone you like? If not, why not? Repeat:

★ **"I am a worthwhile and loving person!"**

★ **"I think you are awesome!"**

★ **"I like you just the way you are!"**

Change or add any other positive affirmations that will make you feel tingly and excited inside.

A Landmark Study

AT THE UNIVERSITY OF California at Berkeley, Professor John A. Clausen, Ph.D., conducted a first-time research project to determine why some people have a considerably better chance of success when facing adulthood. He tracked the lives of three hundred people over a period of fifty years from various ages of five, six and seven until they were fifty-five, fifty-six and fifty-seven.

The evidence that Professor Clausen gathered showed that if a child possessed three specific attributes by the age of eleven his or her chance for success was reasonably assured. The three traits are: <u>self-confidence, dependability and intellectual curiosity.</u>

Though you may be past eleven years old, our advice would be to work to acquire these three qualities as you advance into adulthood. If you have taken this book seriously and done all the Experiments, you surely have an excellent chance of developing self-confidence, dependability and intellectual curiosity.

We hope the following poem will be one that you will live by for the rest of your life.

<u>The Man in the Glass</u>

When you get what you want in your struggle for self
    And the world makes you king for a day
Just go to a mirror and look at yourself
    And see what *that* man has to say.

For it isn't your father, mother or wife
    Whose judgment upon you must pass;
The fellow whose verdict counts most in your life,
    Is the one staring back from the glass.

Some people may think you're a straight-shootin' chum
    And call you a wonderful guy.
But the man in the glass says you're only a bum
    If you can't look him straight in the eye.

He's the fellow to please—never mind all the rest,
    For he's with you clear up to the end.
And you've passed your most dangerous, difficult test
    If the man in the glass is your friend.

You may fool the whole world down the pathway of life,
    And get pats on your back as you pass.
But your final reward will be heartaches and tears,
    If you've cheated the man in the glass!

(Author Unknown)

An Added Surprise

IF YOU RECALL at the beginning of the book, we invited you to write us. We want to know what you think of the book. What do you like about it? What specifically helped you? How has it influenced you? Do you have any suggestions for improving it that you think will help others like yourself? Did you set and achieve at least one goal? Are you proud enough of what you accomplished to share it with us? Because here is the *surprise*:

Prizes will be awarded to the twenty-five best stories we receive! We plan to write another book, only the next time it will consist of success stories about you and other teenagers. Besides including your story with your name and your picture, all twenty-five selected will receive a prize. It will be an autographed copy of, "*More Winners for Life — Teenagers Who Have Learned to Set and Achieve Their Goals!*" The grand prize winner will be selected by a panel of judges and will receive something in addition to what we have mentioned — something valuable and worth shooting for.

Please let us hear from <u>you</u>. And always remember,

WE WANT THE BEST FOR YOU BECAUSE WE BELIEVE YOU ARE THE BEST AND YOU DESERVE THE BEST!

— Donny & Linkie

Write to:
Donny & Linkie   P.O. Box 12161 Dallas, TX 75225

NOTES TO MYSELF

About the Authors

DONNY ANDERSON is a recognizable personality, especially with sports fans. He was two-time All American at Texas Tech; the number one draft choice of the Houston Oilers and Green Bay Packers; played in the Pro Bowl in 1968; played in the first and second Superbowl Playoffs with Coach Vincent T. Lombardi's Green Bay Packers; and he is the current chairman of the National Football League Alumni which represents thirty-three chapters across America.

Donny has two children, both teenagers at this writing, which partly explains his interest in and commitment to writing *Winners for Life*. He has devoted twenty-three years of his life having a wonderful time teaching and coaching youngsters. Among those who have benefited from Donny's efforts are the Special Olympics, Boys and Girls Clubs, The Gatlin Brothers' Gold Tournament, The Jerry Lewis Muscular Dystrophy event, Foster Kids, Underprivileged Youth, Stars for Children Abuse Center and the Big Brothers/Big Sisters Organization.

Donny has given over 2,000 free speeches at schools all over Texas. Today Donny is a scratch golfer, currently playing in the Celebrity Golf Tour. He is an independent insurance agent as well.

LINKIE SELTZER COHN also spent many years working with youngsters. Though her three children are teenagers no longer, while they were growing up Linkie participated wherever they were — from den mother to both the Girls and Boys Scouts, public school and religious school involvement, to sponsoring her children's social groups as well.

She initiated Human Relations Commissions in the Dallas Independent School District while working with the Greater Dallas Human Relations Commission. She also served on their board.

Linkie was nominated for the prestigious Dallas Linz Award for her many volunteer contributions to the city over the years. She was chosen to serve as a judge for the city's annual Teenage Citizenship Tribute award.

Career-wise she taught in Dallas community colleges for seven years; was Executive Director of Friends of the Hebrew University; a professional dancer, then speaker, belonging to National Speakers Association. Today she owns and operates Speakers Source International, booking celebrities, professional speakers and entertainers for corporate and association meetings.

Having belonged to many professional associations through the years, currently Linkie is a member of the International Group of Agencies and Bureaus. She is listed in Who's Who of International Women, Who's Who in the Southwest and Who's Who in the World.

A Secret of Winners

ANOTHER DIFFERENCE BETWEEN *winners* and losers is that *winners* have learned to handle their fears. They are aware of their thoughts, emotions and especially their fears. You can learn to do the same thing.

If you understand that everything begins in your conscious mind, you have the choice of controlling your thoughts. You can choose to think negatively or optimistically. You can choose to think fearful thoughts or cheerful thoughts.

Your thoughts have the power to influence your entire life. In fact, <u>what you think about expands</u>. You may want to read that sentence over again until you fully understand how that can impact you. This is one of the most significant statements in this book. It is the secret of most *winners*. **What you think about expands!**

In other words, your thoughts can forecast what you become. So . . .

> *IF YOU THINK YOU ARE A LOSER, YOU WILL BECOME A LOSER. IF YOU THINK YOU ARE A WINNER, YOU WILL BECOME A WINNER!*   — Donny & Linkie

Introducing you now to . . .

Winny the Winner

You will discover this stout-hearted, playful yet concerned lion is everywhere. Consider Winny to be your mascot, your friend, someone else who cares about you — who wants you to become a *winner!*

What Part Does Fear Play in Your Life?

ALMOST EVERYONE HAS EXPERIENCED feelings of fear at some point in their life. We know few people who haven't felt rejected, self-doubt, jealous, inferior, inadequate, unworthy, unloved, shame, guilt or lack of confidence sometime during their lifetime.

But the worst feeling of all is believing there is no hope. Without some sense of hope, thinking you cannot do what you dream of, your life may have little meaning.

Start questioning your parents and other adults you know. Ask them if they ever experienced any of the feelings we have just described. Ask them about their dreams. What were their desires and ambitions?

Mom - Dad, what were your dreams?

Ask them if they came true. If they didn't, ask them why not. If they didn't achieve their dreams and goals, are you willing to repeat what they did?

What to Do About Fear

WHEN WE STOP TO EXAMINE what we really fear, experts say that we are afraid we are not capable of handling what may come our way. Check it out right now. Think of something that you're afraid of. What do you think is causing your fear? Why not put this book down for a moment and think about that question. What is causing you to feel the fear you are feeling?

Do you think it is because of what someone else did or said? Do you tend to blame others for your problems and fears? If you do, then what part do you play in your fear?

Until you are willing to accept the responsibility for your feelings of fear, how can you possibly get rid of your fears? You are the one who is fearful.

WHO WILL BE IN CONTROL OF FEAR — YOU OR YOUR FEAR?
                                                    — Donny & Linkie

You Can Get Relief

EVENTUALLY YOU WILL learn from your own experience that it is better to work through your fears, to move forward into action than to do nothing. By doing something, even if it doesn't turn out exactly as you want, at least you will know that <u>you did the best you could with the information you had at the time.</u>

Be forewarned — you can expect to be faced with many scary situations simply because you are a teenager. This is a time in your life when you will encounter many new experiences. Doing something for the first time is usually scary, at least it was for us when we were your age. We remember how intimidating it was, how we were afraid we would do something stupid and make fools of ourselves. Many times we did. But we survived, and so will you.

Fear can become one of your best friends if you meet each incident with action. Begin by asking yourself:

Once you answer that question, you will be able to conquer your fears. As a result, you will be able to feel a sense of self-confidence new to you. Your self-esteem is bound to increase. We only wish someone would have explained this to us when we were your age.

> *"I AM NEVER AFRAID OF WHAT I KNOW."*
> — Anna Sewell, English writer

Here Is Your Challenge — EXPERIMENTS

AT THE END OF the chapters you will find two experiments — each for you to sample, to explore, to try out, to see if you receive some benefit.

The first Experiment is an "Action Step." The second Experiment relates to "Affirmations." If you've never heard that word, it means to say something positive.

EXPERIMENT #1
ACTION STEP

THIS EXPERIMENT IS DESIGNED to help you handle your fears. It is important to know that all fears act the same way. It's like putting on a pair of glasses that exaggerate everything and make things look worse.

The first step in confronting your fears is to be very still. Take stock of your body. Be quiet long enough to become aware of the different sensations in your body. You might feel cold or hot, shaky or tingly, an ache here or there. Check your heart. Is it beating fast, slow, rhythmically, or does it feel heavy? Do you feel like laughing? Laughter sometimes disguises fear. Simply becoming aware of what is happening *inside* you is another step in facing fear.

Next, examine the thoughts going on in your head. You will probably get several messages, but the most important one might be, "*I am afraid.*" Again, take the time to think. Think about a situation when you felt like a *winner* — you felt good about something you did in your past.

Now that you feel good about yourself, fill in the following chart. Start writing down everything you can think of that you fear. Then one by one ask, "*What's the worst thing that can happen?*" Answer that question and come up with solutions to deal with each fear. If you stay with this Experiment long enough, you are bound to find answers to conquer some, if not all of your fears.

FEAR	SOLUTION

Resolution: __I will__

Experiment #2
Affirmations

WE HAVE EXPLAINED that an "Affirmation" is an optimistic statement. It is best to say out loud when you are alone. Today, experiment by repeating the following Affirmations before breakfast, lunch and bedtime. From our experience, we can tell you that repeating Affirmations is powerful. It is another way to keep fearful thoughts out of your head. It also is a way to retrain your mind.

★ **"I am handling my fears now!"**

★ **"I am handling whatever comes my way now!"**

★ **"I am accomplishing my goals now!"**

If you are not comfortable with these particular Affirmations, add to, alter or make up your own. We recommend the following guidelines:

1. **Begin with "I am."**

2. **Use an active verb, a word usually ending in "ing."**

3. **End the sentence with the word "now."**

If that doesn't work, then say something that makes you feel good about you. Whichever you choose, be sure to say your Affirmations with enthusiasm and conviction. Keep changing them until you can feel that way.

We started this chapter with Eleanor Roosevelt's quote, *"The future belongs to those who believe in the beauty of their dreams."* To end this chapter, consider this:

> **THE FUTURE BELONGS TO THOSE WHO HAVE DREAMS AND GOALS, AND ARE WILLING TO WORK TO ACHIEVE THEM.** — Donny & Linkie

Answer: The president's name was Abraham Lincoln.

2 Choosing Goals

The Secret to Happiness

> *"KEEP AWAY FROM PEOPLE WHO TRY TO BELITTLE YOUR AMBITIONS. SMALL PEOPLE ALWAYS DO THAT, BUT THE REALLY GREAT MAKE YOU FEEL THAT YOU, TOO, CAN BECOME GREAT."* — Mark Twain

The Game of Life

LIVING LIFE SUCCESSFULLY is not an accident. Life is a game — a skill. It can be learned, just as you can learn to play soccer, dance, read, add or subtract. There are certain rules and guidelines to follow in order to win. If you are willing to learn a new set of skills, then you can devise a game plan that will help you become a *Winner for Life.*

One of the first steps in your game plan could be to follow Mark Twain's advice. If you hang out with people who have no ambition and no goals, besides trying to belittle you, they may even taunt and tease you for wanting to do something that they don't have the guts to do. Why not find people who have the same drive and ambition you do? They will be your cheerleaders, and you can be theirs.

You can count on us to be part of your cheering section as well. Think of us as your coach, like Coach English was to Blake. Our words may push you and maybe even make you angry at times, but always remember, we want you to become a *winner.*

NO MATTER YOUR AGE, YOU ARE NEVER TOO YOUNG TO DREAM, TO IMAGINE, TO HAVE A VISION AND A GOAL. — Donny & Linkie

Time to Release the Past

THIS MAY SURPRISE YOU, but the next step of your game plan is to let go of your past. This minute, imagine you are starting out fresh, relying only on those natural and acquired talents that have benefited you up until now.

What really counts is <u>who you are today</u>, and <u>what you want to accomplish in your future</u>.

Think of it this way. Have you ever run a race? It doesn't really matter if you have or not. Just compare releasing your past to running a race. Let's say you are getting ready to run a mile race. In your mind's eye imagine lining up with nine other runners at the starting blocks.

While you are at the starting line waiting for the race to start, it won't help you to concentrate on the races you've won in the past. Thinking of previous races you won or lost will only rob you of the concentration you need to run this one. If you really want to win *this* race, all your thoughts and actions have to be on one thing and one thing only — to break the ribbon at the finish line before any of the other nine contestants.

Are You Ready to See Yourself As a Winner?

VISUALIZE THE END RESULT you want. You can see hundreds of people watching the race; you can hear them cheering you on as you approach the finish line ahead of all the rest; you can see yourself breaking the ribbon; you can feel the big smile on your face and your heart beating hard with happiness; your friends, family and spectators surround you and reach out to touch you; you can hear them congratulating you, the *winner.*

It's the same when you choose a *goal.* If you are serious about setting a goal and achieving it, your thoughts and actions need to be focused on reaching your *Target Goal*.

Were You Born a Success?

WE HAVE NEVER MET anyone who was born a leader, a champion, or a success. Do you know anyone who was born an accomplished musician, a skilled plumber, a great lawyer, or an established *winner*? We would guess you haven't.

These people had to study and practice for years. They worked hard to learn their craft. That is the price everyone must pay for success—hard work.

> *"THE ONLY TIME 'SUCCESS' COMES BEFORE 'WORK' IS IN THE DICTIONARY."* — Vincent Lombardi

A Three-Step Game Plan

HERE ARE THREE more steps to add to your game plan:

1. HAVE FAITH IN YOURSELF

Know that whatever you want in life, no matter how farfetched it may seem right now, having faith in yourself, believing you can achieve what you want, will propel you toward reaching your *Target Goal*.

Know that we believe in you. We believe you can accomplish anything you truly want, no matter what has happened in the past.

> *"YOU HAVE GREATNESS WITHIN YOU AND YOU HAVE THE POWER TO LIVE YOUR DREAMS."* — Les Brown

2. DISCOVER WHAT YOU LOVE TO DO

This is probably one of the most difficult things that anyone can do. However, the experiment at the end of this chapter will help you discover interests you might not have considered.

The key issue is to choose something that stirs a passion in your heart, like Walt Disney did. Be certain that you would rather do that one thing more than anything else in the world. Then, become "the" expert — study it, practice it, work at it. Know more about it and do it better than anyone else in that field.

> **"I'D RATHER BE A FAILURE AT SOMETHING I ENJOY THAN A SUCCESS AT SOMETHING I HATE."**
> — George Burns, Famous Comedian

3. CHOOSE TO BENEFIT HUMANKIND

If you are like most teenagers, having money is important to you. That's perfectly acceptable — most people want money. But earning money need not be your driving force. Doing what makes you feel electrified and satisfied because you are doing what you love to do, *that* needs to be your driving force. Be assured that . . .

> **MONEY WILL RESULT IF YOU CHOOSE SOMETHING THAT NOT ONLY BENEFITS YOU, BUT OTHER PEOPLE AND THE UNIVERSE AS WELL.** — Donny & Linkie

Can You Aim and Hit the Bull's Eye?

ONCE YOU HAVE some of your desires written down, you will want to select the one that appeals to you the most. We call that a ***Target Goal.***

Here's an example of what we mean when we say ***Target Goal.*** Let's say you are playing a game of darts with a friend. Both of you want to win. Both of you know that the one who hits the bull's eye most often will be the victor. So hitting the bull's eye becomes your ***Target Goal.***

When it's your turn, will you try to throw the dart closest to the bull's eye or will you aim somewhere else on the dart board? We know you are smart enough, especially because you are reading this book, to always aim for the bull's eye.

The same is true about goal setting. When you decide on a goal you want to achieve, the idea is to always go for the end result, the bull's eye, the ***target.***

<u>Supporting Steps</u>

BY NOW YOU ARE AWARE that in order to reach your *target* you have to move into action. We call this action *Supporting Steps*. For example, let's say you want to go to a football game tonight, which becomes your ***Target Goal***. Consider what it will take to get there.

What's the first thing you need? Wouldn't it be money so you can buy the ticket? Do you ask your parents, work to get enough money, or save your allowance to buy the ticket? Next you have to find a way of getting to the football stadium.

You arrange all of that and arrive at your destination. You are sitting down ready to watch the game feeling satisfied that you have finally reached your ***Target Goal.*** Everything else you did to get to the game were *Supporting Steps.*

Do you understand the difference between ***Target Goals*** and *Supporting Steps*? The ***Target Goal*** is the end result, while the *Supporting Steps* help you achieve your final result.

HERE'S TO YOUR SUCCESS!!

"THE DIFFERENCE BETWEEN THE IMPOSSIBLE AND POSSIBLE LIES IN A PERSON'S DETERMINATION"
— Tommy Lasorda
Coach, Los Angeles Dodgers Baseball Team

EXPERIMENT #3
ACTION STEP

BEFORE YOU READ THIS Experiment we want to explain Core Beliefs*. Core Beliefs originate in your heart. They are the very essence and core of who you are as a person. These beliefs are the foundation of all of the experiences that have affected you from birth until now. Core Beliefs are a result of the influence of those who have reared you, your friends, people in your religious and educational institutions, plus others who have made an impression on you.

By knowing what your Core Beliefs are, you can become aware of what actually motivates you, what mobilizes your spirit and energy into action. With this understanding, you can function at your highest level so that you can accomplish what you want in life.

---

*The Core Belief Exercise was developed by Juanell Teague, a coach to speakers and corporate leaders, and Glenna Salsbury, a professional speaker.

CORE BELIEFS

___	Money	___	___	Competition ___
___	Recognition	___	___	Cleanliness ___
___	Independence	___	___	Fame ___
___	Family	___	___	Orderliness ___
___	Adventure	___	___	Productivity ___
___	Structure	___	___	Power ___
___	Punctuality	___	___	Love ___
___	Security	___	___	Peace ___
___	Solitude	___	___	Purpose ___
___	Appreciation	___	___	Faith ___
___	Health	___	___	People ___
___	Creativity	___	___	Service ___
___	Knowledge	___	___	Wisdom ___
___	Challenge	___	___	Cultural ___
___	Excitement	___	___	Activities ___
___	Self Respect	___	___	Other ___

CORE BELIEFS

A. Review the list of Core Beliefs. Then choose the ten that are of most interest to you. Put a check mark on the right side of each of the ten. Remember, this is your list, your decision to make alone. Do not answer the way you think someone else would want you to.

B. From the list of ten that you have just checked, narrow your list to five. Choose carefully and with a lot of thought. Let your heart be your guide. Repeat out loud those ten you have chosen and see what kind of reaction you get from your body before you refine your selection. If you take time to become aware of how your body reacts to various words, you will learn a lot about yourself.

C. Now that you are sure of your top five selections, use the line on the left to number them from one to five. Number one is your top priority.

Why not test your selection over the next few days? Think about each of the five Core Beliefs you have chosen. Put each of them into action. Experience which feels most comfortable. After doing that, change the order if you realize another belief is more important to you. When you begin to select *Target Goals* be sure your Core Beliefs are included, especially your number one choice.

EXPERIMENT #4
AFFIRMATIONS

HERE ARE YOUR Affirmations for Chapter 2. If you choose, say them aloud three times a day — before breakfast in the morning, before lunch at noon, before you go to sleep at night. This time we recommend saying Affirmations each day over the next seven days.

We write our Affirmations on a small piece of paper so we can look at them during different times of the day. You might want to do the same thing. And you might also want to start a Goal-Setting Notebook where your chosen Affirmations and Experiments can be logged.

★ **"I am working to get what I want now!"**

★ **"I am energizing myself by working in line with my core beliefs now!"**

★ **"I am reaching my Target Goal now!"**

Becoming a *winner* begins by writing down one goal. It can be as simple as deciding to read one chapter in a book for a class assignment, or choosing to eat healthy food instead of junk food for a day. Go for something easy to begin with, something you know you can accomplish. We don't want you to feel overwhelmed.

If you run into obstacles along the way, decide what you are willing to do or give up in order to reach your *Target Goal*.

This will be the test to discover how committed you are — how tough you really are — whether or not you will stick in there and persevere until you realize one of your dreams.

"YOU ARE NEVER A LOSER UNTIL YOU STOP TRYING."
— Mike Ditka, Former Football Coach
Television Sports Announcer

NOTES TO MYSELF

3 Setting Goals

The Secret to Getting What You Want

> *"THE PERFECT DISCIPLINED WILL IS TO REFUSE TO ADMIT DEFEAT."* — Vincent Lombardi

<u>Setting Goals Is Easy</u>

IT'S THE ACCOMPLISHMENT that is difficult. There is a woman whose dream came true because she had "Disciplined Will." You may have heard or read about her. Her name is Gail Devers. She trained for years so that she could run in the Olympics. But without warning she was struck down by a disabling illness called Graves Disease.

At one point, the disease had progressed to such an extent that Gail's doctors wanted to amputate both of her feet. But she refused to let them. She wouldn't give up her dream, her goal. She was determined to compete again.

Against all odds, she did. After her miraculous recovery, Gail reached her **Target Goal** primarily because of her Disciplined Will. In the 1992 Summer Olympics she won the Gold Medal for the 100 meter race and the title Gail Devers worked years to achieve, the World's Fastest Woman!

Performing at Your Top

YOUR SUCCESS IN ANY endeavor will include a combination of three other things as well: *your physical readiness, your skill readiness,* and *your psychological readiness.*

PHYSICAL READINESS:

Gail Devers could never have accomplished her goal until she restored herself to health. When you have a healthy body you also have the energy to get whatever you need accomplished. A vigorous body will help you face the stresses and challenges of life as well.

Winning athletes spend endless hours practicing in the justifiable belief that this will improve their performance. It takes study, work and endless hours of practice.

Whether or not you plan to be an athlete, whether or not you have a physical disability, striving to maintain a healthy body by eating nourishing foods and exercising on a regular basis is the fundamental way to establish Physical Readiness. Mentioning the danger of drugs, smoking or alcohol is not necessary, is it?

Donny Anderson — A Winner for Life

DID YOU KNOW THAT Donny Anderson owns two Super Bowl Rings? Donny's dream came true when he played with the Green Bay Packers professional football team under the man who is considered the most outstanding coach of all time, Vincent T. Lombardi. Green Bay won the first two Super Bowl games ever played!

Lombardi became Donny's mentor. He influenced Donny to such an extent that much of what you are reading here is a result of that relationship.

Donny was just seven years old when he envisioned himself as a professional baseball player. As he grew older he changed his focus to become a football player instead.

As a senior in high school during the last football game of the season, Donny broke his neck. Even that didn't keep him from reaching his goal. He recovered more quickly than most because of his determination to start playing football in college. In his senior year at Texas Tech, where he became known as the "Golden Palomino," Donny was the number one draft choice of the Packers. His number was 44.

Lombardi constantly emphasized the gap between skill level and performance level, saying skill level represents *potential* while performance level represents *production*. Lombardi equated production to *results*. The Green Bay Packers produced the results Lombardi demanded. That is why Donny's team won the first two Super Bowls ever played and Donny has not one, but two Super Bowl Rings.

Psychological Readiness:

Psychological Readiness is to the mind what physical fitness is to the body. Learning how to control one's mind is as critical as being able to control one's body. The following stories about W. Mitchell and Charlie Boswell illustrate what it means to be psychologically ready.

W. Mitchell's Miraculous Story

W. MITCHELL HAD NOT ONE, but two disastrous accidents that would have left most people feeling so sorry for themselves that they would have given up on life forever. But not Mitchell.

First, while riding his motorcycle, he was nearly killed in a freak accident that left ninety percent of his body burned. As a result, Mitchell's face is a patchwork of multicolored skin grafts, and the fingers on both hands are missing.

The second accident occurred four years later. He was piloting his private plane when it crashed. Besides suffering a broken back, his legs were paralyzed.

Yet today, Mitchell is a millionaire, a former mayor and Congressional candidate, author, sought-after professional speaker, even a river-rafter and sky diver — plus he married a pretty nurse, as well. Most miraculously, he accomplished all these things *after* both accidents.

By telling his gripping story to thousands of people across the country in person and on public television, he has inspired many to look at their lives again, to start anew if necessary. He encourages everyone to work toward making their dreams come true, just as we are encouraging you.

"IT ISN'T WHAT HAPPENS TO YOU THAT MATTERS. IT IS WHAT YOU DO ABOUT IT." — W. Mitchell

The Charlie Boswell Story

A WINNING-EDGE ATTITUDE changed the destiny of a man you probably have never heard about. His name is Charlie Boswell. His dream as a boy was to become a professional baseball player for the New York Yankees. Unfortunately, World War II was in progress when Charlie graduated from college, so instead he immediately went into the Army. He earned the rank of captain, and left for Germany to head a tank division.

During the fighting, Charlie's group was hit with mortar. All of his men escaped except one. Charlie quickly ran back and climbed into the tank, only to find the driver frozen from fear with his hands still on the wheel.

As quickly as he could, Charlie managed to get the youngster out of the tank to safety. Then another shell exploded. This one hit Charlie.

He woke up three weeks later in a hospital, bandaged from head to toe unable to move. His friends tried to get him out of bed once he was able, but he continually refused. Finally, one of the guys told Charlie, *"We're going to play golf. You've got to get out of this hospital and do something other than lie in that bed. You've got to get a new attitude."*

Charlie's response was, *"I don't like golf."* His friend persisted, *"You are going to play golf with me today."*

The first ball that Charlie Boswell hit was 150 yards straight down the middle of the fairway! That is unusual for a first time golf swing. After that day he decided to go for a different **Target Goal**, promising himself, *"I'm going to become the best golfer I can be."*

Now he is included in the record books. Charlie Boswell has won 22 national *blind* golf championships!

> **"DO NOT LET WHAT YOU CANNOT DO INTERFERE WITH WHAT YOU CAN DO."** — John Wooden

SKILL READINESS:

All of us have been blessed with at least one God-given talent. Perhaps you haven't discovered it yet, but it is somewhere inside you. You have it. Everyone has it. You probably wouldn't guess that it took one of television's top stars many years to develop his "Skill Readiness."

The Superstar Who Quit Twice

IF YOU WERE TO READ the life story of one of the most admired and trusted men in this country, you would discover that Bill Cosby quit school twice in his life. Though he always tested high on intelligence tests, he goofed off through school and dropped out when he didn't know enough to be promoted to the eleventh grade. He joined the Navy rather than face the embarrassment of repeating the same grade.

After a few months he began to notice his Navy buddies were struggling to finish their education. Cosby decided they didn't have as much "upstairs" as he knew he did. He realized he was committing a sin, a mental sin. He decided to start studying so he could earn a high school diploma. He accomplished that *Target Goal* easily.

He Made His Dream Come True First, Then . . .

AFTER HIS NAVAL SERVICE ended, Cosby won an athletic scholarship to Temple University. In order to stay in college, he had to work to support himself. He found a job tending bar at a coffeehouse that featured comedians. His boss recognized Cosby's talent and gave him a break filling in when the professional comic was off.

Cosby worked hard to perfect his jokes and his timing during those years. He would review taped segments of his routines to figure out why the audience laughed at a joke some nights and not on others. He practiced, performed, and reviewed his work. Then he practiced, performed, and reviewed his work again and again and again.

That is exactly what we mean when we refer to *Skill Readiness.* When the opportunity came, Cosby's skill as a comic was primed. He was ready to perform.

He Became an Educated Man

EVENTUALLY COSBY'S BOSS hired him to perform regularly and he earned more money than ever before. That's when he decided to drop out of school a second time.

Today Bill Cosby is considered one of the most talented, respected and distinguished entertainers in the country. More to his credit, he not only completed his college degree, but he earned a Ph.D. in Education as well. Cosby has given away millions of dollars to educational institutions to assist deserving students because he understands the importance of a college education.

What Is The Winning Edge?

WHAT MADE W. MITCHELL and Charlie Boswell winners? It is simple. Instead of thinking about the ten thousand and one things they *cannot* do, they concentrate on the one thousand and one things that they *can* do. They set goals for themselves and achieved them because of their optimistic, determined attitude. So now you know that the ***Winning Edge*** is your <u>attitude</u>.

Your attitude will direct your life. With a "will do" optimistic, disciplined attitude your life can be an adventure, fun and fulfilling. Next to your relationship with whomever you believe is the Highest Power, your relationship with *you*, knowing you can count on *you* no matter the circumstances, is the way you can have the ***Winning Edge.***

How to Develop that Attitude

IF YOU WANT TO KNOW how to develop a **Winning Edge** attitude, here is one way to begin. First, put a rubber band on your wrist that is tight enough so you know that it is there.

Next, begin to monitor your thoughts for one hour. Become aware of what you are thinking. Each time you find yourself thinking about something in a negative way, snap that rubber band.

Gradually start monitoring your thoughts for two hours, then four hours, until you are able to be aware of your thoughts for an entire day. Stretch the rubber band and release it whenever you are not thinking optimistically.

**Conscious Mind:
Think Optimistically**

Before you go to sleep at night, look at your wrist. If your wrist is sore and your skin is red, that means you must have snapped that rubber band a lot. You must have been thinking negative thoughts throughout the day. If your skin is not blemished, that means you must have had optimistic thoughts that day. That is what you want to achieve.

Continually feed your mind with healthy, optimistic thoughts just as you feed your body healthy, nourishing food to stay robust and fit. Read uplifting books. Listen to music and tapes that have inspiring messages, that make you feel good. Your local library keeps a supply without cost.

Another help to developing a *winning attitude* is to repeat your Affirmations at least three times daily. Consciously direct a steady stream of constructive messages toward the outcomes you <u>want</u> rather than the outcomes you <u>fear</u>.

Attitude

"THE LONGER I LIVE, the more I realize the impact of attitude on life. Attitude, to me, is more important than facts.

It is more important than the past, than education, than money, than circumstances, than failures, than successes, than what other people think or say or do.

It is more important than appearance, giftedness or skill. It will make or break a company...a church...a home.

The remarkable thing is we have a choice every day regarding the attitude we will embrace for that day.

We cannot change our past...we cannot change the fact that people will act a certain way. We cannot change the inevitable.

The only thing we can do is play on the one string we have, and that is our attitude...

I am convinced that life is 10% what happens to me and 90% how I react to it.

And so it is with you...we are in charge of our attitudes."

By Charles Swindoll

Two Lessons from Pain

BOTH OF US HAVE HAD our share of successes and failures the same as Bill Cosby. Winning was fun. The failures were not. They caused us pain. We learned two valuable lessons from that pain. The first lesson is . . .

☞ **It always takes longer than expected to reach a goal.**

For example, this book took over three years to complete. We never imagined it would take that long. So be prepared to persevere long enough until you succeed. If, after <u>all</u> your efforts don't work, move forward with a lesson learned never to repeat again.

The second lesson was a surprise. At the time of failure it doesn't seem possible that anything positive can happen. But over the years, and only in looking back, have we learned from our pain that . . .

☞ **Something good comes from every failure.**

NOTHING IS AS PAINFUL AS THE LOSS OF UNFULFILLED DREAMS. — Donny and Linkie

The Concept of Achievement

THE ENTIRE CONCEPT of achievement is based on setting goals. When you set goals for yourself, you become a more spirited, enthusiastic and focused individual. Life is more fun.

Most of us fail more often than we succeed. Abraham Lincoln was a prime example. He failed twelve times over twenty-nine years before he was elected president.

Accept the fact that it's not so dreadful to fail. You won't have to disappear off the face of the earth if you make a mistake. We bet your friends won't desert you, neither will your family, and neither will we. But think of the other side of the coin. What if you set a goal and you succeed? What could be more fulfilling and exciting?

We certainly don't expect you to be perfect, so please don't try. All of us are only human. Humans weren't created to be perfect.

YOU WERE BORN TO GROW, TO LEARN, TO CREATE, EXPERIENCE LOVE AND JOY, AND SHARE YOUR UNIQUE TALENTS WITH THE WORLD.
— Donny and Linkie

EXPERIMENT #5
ACTION PLAN

AT THE END OF Chapter 2, you rated your Core Values. From your final list of five, decide which one you want to choose for a **Target Goal**. Be sure you feel totally committed to whichever you choose. Know that your heart, and not your head, is directing you to this one goal. Next . . .

ACTION PLAN

1. Target Goal

2. Deadline

3. Supporting Steps

4. My Daily List

1. WRITE YOUR GOAL DOWN

Fill in the Action Plan on the next page.

2. SET A DATE FOR THE ACCOMPLISHMENT

Select the date that you want to complete your goal. Don't rush yourself. There's no need to pressure yourself any more than you are right now. Remember, be kind to yourself. You deserve it.

3. SUPPORTING STEPS

List all the steps you can think of that will support and help you reach your **Target Goal.** To review *Supporting Steps* turn back to page 36 in Chapter 2.

4. MY DAILY LIST

Fill in "My Daily List" on the next page. Divide the list of things you want to do between daytime and evening hours. In the lower right-hand box, write your name in the blank space following, "Something that gives me, (*your name*), satisfaction."

Think about what simple, everyday pleasures give you satisfaction and include them here. Maybe being with friends, or playing with your pet gives you pleasure. Or perhaps making good grades or doing something nice for someone else gives you a lot of enjoyment. The idea is to get used to thinking about and doing things that make you feel good about you.

In the lower left-hand corner, write a commitment to yourself. Example, *"I promise to work toward my **Target Goal** each day."* Then do what it takes to keep from disappointing yourself.

ACTION PLAN

Name: _____ Today's Date: _____

Target Goal: _____

Date to be completed: _____

My Daily List

Supporting Steps/Daytime	Supporting Steps/Evening

My commitment to me:	Something that gives me,
	_____,
	(name)
	satisfaction:

EXPERIMENT #6
AFFIRMATIONS

★ **I am becoming a winner now!**

★ **I am visualizing my Target Goal now!**

★ **I am persevering until I accomplish my goal**

of _____

_____**now!**

(fill in this blank)

Close Your Mouth

NOW THAT YOU HAVE COMPLETED these two pages, don't tell a soul. There is a power within you that will cooperate and help you achieve your goals if you will just keep it to yourself. Start learning to trust yourself, to have faith in yourself and your personal power. You really can do it. We know you can.

A VISION WITHOUT PREPARATION, PLANNING AND PERFORMANCE IS JUST ANOTHER DAYDREAM.
— **Donny & Linkie**

NOTES TO MYSELF

4 Achieving Goals

The Secret to Belonging

A GOAL IS A DREAM WITH A DEADLINE.
                                    — Donny & Linkie

The Unique You

ARE YOU AWARE OF HOW precious you are? Yes, we mean you! You are not only a special individual, but you were born a *winner*. You are unique and different from every other person in the entire world and here's the proof:

☞ Your physical structure, your facial features, even your hair is different from any one you know, right?

☞ No one else has your set of fingerprints. The police, F.B.I., and other government agencies use fingerprints for identifying individuals suspected of crimes.

☞ Scientists have discovered another method for identifying individuals, called DNA profiling. DNA stands for deoxyribonucleic acid, and is found in blood, bone, hair and semen.

☞ No one else has the same vocal tonality that you have. In fact, you may be identifying yourself through your voice rather than a driver's license in the near future.

☞ For you to have been born, you had to battle fifty million other sperm who were fighting to be born at the same time as you. *You* conquered every obstacle. *You* persevered. *You won out!*

So what does all of this prove? First, it proves that you began life as a *winner*. So why would you want to be anything other than a *winner*? Secondly, you have the potential to offer something original to contribute to the world that no one else can.

I began a WINNER.
I am still a WINNER!

Check out Your Success Factor

SURELY BY NOW YOU KNOW how we feel about you. Take this opportunity to find out how you feel about yourself. It is all about self-esteem.

How high or low is your self-esteem, your feeling of self-worth? No one else can answer that. It is your call.

You can decide that you are a valuable, respectable, lovable, competent, worthwhile and important human being who agrees with us, or you can decide the exact opposite — all negative traits and qualities not worth putting on this paper.

If you are interested in finding out how you actually feel about yourself, answer the following questions. Give serious thought to each one before checking "yes" or "no."

Self-Esteem Questionnaire

<u>Yes</u> <u>No</u> <u>Do You Consider Yourself to Be:</u>

__ __ 1. Fun to be with?

__ __ 2. A good friend?

__ __ 3. Smart?

__ __ 4. Level headed?

__ __ 5. A positive role-model?

__ __ 6. Attractive?

__ __ 7. Worthwhile?

__ __ 8. Acceptable to others?

__ __ 9. Generous?

__ __ 10. Tolerant of others not like you?

__ __ 11. Trustworthy?

__ __ 12. Able to trust others?

__ __ 13. Honest about your feelings?

__ __ 14. Able to share your feelings?

__ __ 15. Dependable?

__ __ 16. Willing to learn from your mistakes?

__ __ 17. Able to accept criticism comfortably?

__ __ 18. Flexible — willing to change?

__ __ 19. Developing your talents?

__ __ 20. Happy for others when they succeed?

__ __ 21. Able to accept your shortcomings?

__ __ 22. Loyal?

Yes	No	**Do You Consider Yourself to Be:**
___	___	23. Self disciplined?
___	___	24. Goal oriented?
___	___	25. Able to give love?
___	___	26. Accountable for your actions?
___	___	27. Kind?

Yes	No	**Is It Easy for You To:**
___	___	28. Make new friends?
___	___	29. Accept your love?
___	___	30. Praise others?
___	___	31. Praise yourself?
___	___	32. Laugh at yourself?
___	___	33. Say, *"No!"* to peers when your gut says to?
___	___	34. Admit to making a mistake?
___	___	35. Develop your strengths?
___	___	36. Be friends with those not like you?

Yes	No	**Do You:**
___	___	37. Like yourself?
___	___	38. Trust yourself?
___	___	39. Respect who you are?
___	___	40. Feel confident about your abilities?
___	___	41. Give yourself credit when you deserve it?

<u>Yes</u> <u>No</u>   <u>Do You:</u>

___ ___   42. Encourage yourself to be your best?

___ ___   43. Encourage others to be their best?

___ ___   44. Feel a sense of responsibility to others?

___ ___   45. Have a sense of humor?

___ ___   46. Take on new challenges?

___ ___   47. Avoid pushing people around?

___ ___   48. Take pride in your achievements?

___ ___   49. Accept responsibility for what you do?

___ ___   50. Have high energy and drive?

___ ___   51. Care about others?

___ ___   52. Work to improve yourself?

___ ___   53. Value your closest relationships?

___ ___   54. Express your appreciation to them?

___ ___   55. Feel great about yourself?

___   **TOTAL** of "Yes" answers only

How Did You Do?

TOTAL YOUR "YES" ANSWERS. If you answered all 55 questions "Yes," your self-esteem is abundantly healthy. There is no need for us to applaud you. You're confident enough not to need outside praise.

Here is a challenge. Each "No" answer is worthy of becoming one of your goals — to turn into a "Yes." Choose one "No" and take as much time as you need to turn it into a "Yes."

Continue until you have all 55 "Yes" answers. Don't give up. Persevere. Owning high self-esteem is critical to your future success and to your becoming a *Winner for Life.*

We would guess that most of you reading this didn't reach that magic number of 55 "Yes" answers. If you had asked either of us to answer these same questions at your age, we can assure you we wouldn't have reached 55 "Yes" answers either. Just don't be discouraged. There is hope.

Do You Know of Dr. Wayne Dyer?

MOST PSYCHOLOGISTS AND psychiatrists agree that it is possible to change how you feel about yourself. Dr. Wayne Dyer, famed psychologist and author states,

> *"I believe almost all human problems stem from low self-esteem, from not liking themselves very much. Fears of failure, poverty, rejection, criticism, loss are all a result of low self-esteem. When you genuinely like and respect yourself as a valuable and worthwhile person, the less you fear failure, because you realize your failures are not you. The less you fear rejection, the less you are concerned with what people like or dislike about you, and the more willing you are to reach out to fulfilling your full potential."*

Realize that you can become a person with high self-esteem. You can *make* it happen by being active, creative and mentally tough. Remember, you are becoming what you think about every minute of the day. Focus on your desires. Focus on your *Target Goals.* <u>Act</u> to make them come true.

<u>Could You Give One Hundred Dollars Away?</u>

OWNING HIGH SELF-ESTEEM allows you to like yourself. Eventually you even will be able to love yourself. When you love yourself, you can be more caring, kinder and respectful to others. You are probably wondering what we mean.

Think about it this way. If you wanted to give your best friend a ticket to a concert, or a compact disc, or hundred dollars, those things would have to belong to you. You would have to own them before you could give them away. Right? But then you most likely would want to keep the hundred dollars, so use your imagination for this one.

The same applies to love. If you don't love yourself first, then how can you give your love away to someone else? On that same note, how can you have good feelings about people if you don't own good feelings toward yourself first?

Love Yourself

WHEN YOU LOVE YOURSELF, IT'S EASIER TO FEEL YOU DESERVE TO BE A WINNER IN LIFE. — Donny & Linkie

Know Someone Who Boasts Too Much?

PLEASE UNDERSTAND. When we talk about loving yourself, we are not talking about being cocky or conceited. You know lots of people like that we're sure. They probably have a poor self-image and low self-esteem. They try to cover it up by going to the opposite extreme of bragging and boasting.

There is another kind of person you know as well. We are referring to the person who puts you down or criticizes you. They try to humiliate you, embarrass you and make you feel bad about yourself.

This is just another example of a person with low self-esteem. When they are putting you <u>down</u>, they feel <u>up</u>. It's their way of making themselves feel important. It's also their way of getting attention. These are usually unsuccessful people who, when they are not thinking about themselves, are thinking about lack, loss, limitation and how much everything costs.

What's Showing When You Apply for a Job?

WHEN YOU GET READY to go into the marketplace to apply for a job, realize your self-esteem will be showing. How you feel about yourself will be reflected in the way you walk, the way you talk, the way you sit or stand. Every move you make will tell the other person what you think of yourself. When you have high self-esteem, you can almost touch it. If you have low self-esteem, it is evident as well.

High self-esteem has recently been added to the list of qualities that companies want and expect their employees to have.

Employers today consider it a basic skill that is just as important as reading, writing and math. Three other qualifications employers look for are:

1. Attitude: They want someone who is enthusiastic, easy to get along with, willing to learn and work hard.

2. Education: They prefer a college graduate, but a high school diploma is a must.

3. Experience: Employers want someone who is industrious; who has worked somewhere before they come to apply to them.

A Critical Time for Choices

WE ARE STRESSING the importance of feeling good about yourself because we want you to have all the tools you need to accomplish your *Target Goals* now!

This is a critical stage in your life. Deciding to graduate from high school and hopefully college are two of the most important decisions you will make. That is why we chose to write this book for your particular age group.

We want to think that this book will help you make the right choices not only for your future, but also for the future of our country. Don't forget, you are our future leaders. You are needed!

> **THE REST OF YOUR LIFE DEPENDS ON CHOICES YOU MAKE NOW.**
> —Donny & Linkie

Have Fun Choosing a Mentor

TO BE A **WINNER**, it is important to study success. Think of all the people you know. Which of them do you consider to be *winners?* Who would you most want to choose as a role model? Take time to consider that question. Once you make that decision, ask that person to be your mentor.

A mentor is a "wise advisor, a teacher, a friend, a coach." Wouldn't you like to have someone like that in your life? You can. All you have to do is <u>ask</u>.

This person might be a religious leader, a business person, someone important in your community, an older brother or sister, a grandparent, a teacher, or maybe one of your parents or adopted parents.

In our experience, we have found that the more successful people are, the nicer they are. Why? Because they own high self-esteem! They don't feel threatened by anyone, and therefore it is easier for them to be nice to everyone.

It would be wise to choose someone whose career matches your interests. Meet with them on a regular basis. Listen to them. Study them. Ask them to tell you their story.

Ask about their failures as well as their successes. Together, strategize your future. Learn everything you can from them.

Here Is a Warning

BE PREPARED FOR rejection. The person you ask may refuse your request. Why? Because they are *winners* and *winners* are constantly striving for higher goals as well as helping others. They may not have enough time for you right now. Just don't take it personally.

Be bold; be courageous. Keep asking. Even if it takes five, six or even ten tries before you get a *"yes."* Don't give up. Persevere. Even if you don't feel like a *winner* to start with, if you will act like a *winner*, do the same things that other *winners* do, you eventually will begin to feel self-confident, competent and unafraid of anything. You might want to check out Experiment #7 at the end of this chapter before you ask someone to be your mentor.

"NEVER GIVE IN. NEVER GIVE IN. NEVER. NEVER. NEVER. NEVER IN ANYTHING GREAT OR SMALL, LARGE OR PETTY; NEVER GIVE IN EXCEPT TO CONVICTIONS OF HONOR AND GOOD SENSE."
— **Winston Churchill**
Prime Minister, England

The Woman Who Gave Up Too Soon

THIS STORY IS ABOUT a woman who would never give in. Her name is Florence Chadwick. At twenty-four years of age she was a world-renowned long distance swimmer. Florence broke all existing records for swimming the English Channel from both directions. In the summer of 1952, she decided to swim twenty-two miles of the Catalina Channel in California.

The day of the event the area was blanketed by fog. As millions of people watched from the shoreline and on their television sets, Florence waded into the water. Hour after hour ticked off as she fought bone-chilling cold, fog and shark infested waters. Several times sharks had to be driven away with rifle shots to keep her from being eaten alive.

She became desperate as she tried to make out the shoreline through her swimmer's goggles. After fifteen hours and fifty-five minutes, frozen to the bone, she asked to be pulled into the boat. Once ashore Chadwick was heartbroken to learn she was only one-half mile from her **Target Goal.** She told the news reporters, *"If I could have seen land, I know I could have made it."*

Determined not to quit a loser, two months later she swam the same channel blanketed by fog, as before. Only this time she made it.

Are you wondering what changed? It was her *Winning-Edge Attitude*. She didn't let the fog defeat her. Chadwick swam with the picture of land firmly entrenched in her mind, and the faith in her heart that she could make it to shore.

Not only was Florence Chadwick the first woman to swim the Catalina Channel, she also beat the men's record by two hours!

Worth Repeating!

PLEASE GIVE YOURSELF the best chance you can in life. Believe in yourself. Let your dreams, desires, visions, goals become a reality. Be all that you can be. If a goal has come into your mind, you are bound to have the ability necessary to accomplish it.

Be accountable to yourself. Once you make a decision to do something, don't disappoint yourself. Upon accomplishment, reward yourself. Be kind to yourself, you deserve it. Life is not a constant win or lose battle. It is full of challenges and opportunities.

> *YOU ARE AN IMPORTANT PART OF THIS UNIVERSE. WITHOUT YOU, THERE WOULD BE AN IRREPLACEABLE VOID.* — Donny & Linkie

Experiment #7
Action Step

THIS ACTION STEP IS going to be a game — one you play by yourself, against yourself. Go back to the Self-Esteem Questionnaire and read number 30. Do you know how to praise others? Do you ever do it? Since we know few adults who praise others, you probably never had anyone to copy. To play the game follow the instructions below:

1. Select seven people you like a lot. Try including one or two adults.

2. Write their names in the "Self-Esteem Game" form on page 79.

3. Decide whether each one has "high" or "low," self-esteem. Mark your answer under "Your Guess."

4. Next, praise each of the seven. Be sure the two of you are alone at the time you are ready to praise them.

I have HIGH self-esteem.

I want you to have high self-esteem too!

EXPERIMENT #7
ACTION STEP

5. After you have given your praise, stand still with your eyes wide open and examine their reaction. <u>The first thirty seconds is critical</u>. Watch carefully their facial and body reactions. If they look at you as if they don't believe you, you will know that they probably have "low" self-esteem. If they start laughing, or make fun of you, or say something like, '*You've got to be kidding*," can you guess where their self-esteem is? Wouldn't you guess "low?" We would.

   However, if they accept your words easily, smile and even say "*Thank you*," you know that person surely has a sense of "high" self-esteem.

6. To score, match your first answer with the one you chose after you praised them Count how many you got right. <u>To win the game you have to guess all seven correctly.</u>

The key to this game will be your sincerity. Avoid complementing/praising/validating your friends about their looks or their clothes. You can use the Self-Esteem Game to pick out qualities that fit them if you can't think of anything else to say. We promise if you are serious and sincere when you validate your seven, they will have to believe what you are saying about them.

We hope you will keep playing this game until you do get seven correct answers. Then keep validating people. Seek out someone each day of the week. Make it a habit. If you want to feel like you "belong" this is one sure way to get there.

THE SELF-ESTEEM GAME

NAME	YOUR GUESS: HIGH LOW		ACTUAL RESULT: HIGH LOW	
1.				
2.				
3.				
4.				
5.				
6.				
7.				

After you have completed this game take stock of yourself. See if you feel any differently about yourself than you did before you started. Our guess is that you will feel better about yourself. Why? First, because you chose a goal and completed it; second, because you helped someone else feel good about themselves. That will surely make you feel good about yourself.

Start praising others regularly. It is another way to increase your self-esteem. By the way, when you find someone with high self-esteem, you may want to be around that person as often as possible.

EXPERIMENT #8

AFFIRMATIONS

BEGIN SAYING THESE Affirmations in the morning when you are brushing your teeth and looking into the mirror. Take forty-two seconds longer to look at yourself — we mean *really* look at yourself. Who do you see? Is it someone you like? If not, why not? Repeat:

★ **"I am a worthwhile and loving person!"**

★ **"I think you are awesome!"**

★ **"I like you just the way you are!"**

Change or add any other positive affirmations that will make you feel tingly and excited inside.

A Landmark Study

AT THE UNIVERSITY OF California at Berkeley, Professor John A. Clausen, Ph.D., conducted a first-time research project to determine why some people have a considerably better chance of success when facing adulthood. He tracked the lives of three hundred people over a period of fifty years from various ages of five, six and seven until they were fifty-five, fifty-six and fifty-seven.

The evidence that Professor Clausen gathered showed that if a child possessed three specific attributes by the age of eleven his or her chance for success was reasonably assured. The three traits are: <u>self-confidence, dependability and intellectual curiosity.</u>

Though you may be past eleven years old, our advice would be to work to acquire these three qualities as you advance into adulthood. If you have taken this book seriously and done all the Experiments, you surely have an excellent chance of developing self-confidence, dependability and intellectual curiosity.

We hope the following poem will be one that you will live by for the rest of your life.

<u>The Man in the Glass</u>

When you get what you want in your struggle for self
    And the world makes you king for a day
Just go to a mirror and look at yourself
    And see what that man has to say.

For it isn't your father, mother or wife
    Whose judgment upon you must pass;
The fellow whose verdict counts most in your life,
    Is the one staring back from the glass.

Some people may think you're a straight-shootin' chum
    And call you a wonderful guy.
But the man in the glass says you're only a bum
    If you can't look him straight in the eye.

He's the fellow to please—never mind all the rest,
    For he's with you clear up to the end.
And you've passed your most dangerous, difficult test
    If the man in the glass is your friend.

You may fool the whole world down the pathway of life,
    And get pats on your back as you pass.
But your final reward will be heartaches and tears,
    If you've cheated the man in the glass!

(Author Unknown)

An Added Surprise

IF YOU RECALL at the beginning of the book, we invited you to write us. We want to know what you think of the book. What do you like about it? What specifically helped you ? How has it influenced you? Do you have any suggestions for improving it that you think will help others like yourself? Did you set and achieve at least one goal? Are you proud enough of what you accomplished to share it with us? Because here is the *surprise*:

Prizes will be awarded to the twenty-five best stories we receive! We plan to write another book, only the next time it will consist of success stories about you and other teenagers. Besides including your story with your name and your picture, all twenty-five selected will receive a prize. It will be an autographed copy of, "*More Winners for Life — Teenagers Who Have Learned to Set and Achieve Their Goals!*" The grand prize winner will be selected by a panel of judges and will receive something in addition to what we have mentioned — something valuable and worth shooting for.

Please let us hear from <u>you</u>. And always remember,

WE WANT THE BEST FOR YOU BECAUSE WE BELIEVE YOU ARE THE BEST AND YOU DESERVE THE BEST!

— Donny & Linkie

Write to:
Donny & Linkie   P.O. Box 12161   Dallas, TX 75225

NOTES TO MYSELF

About the Authors

DONNY ANDERSON is a recognizable personality, especially with sports fans. He was two-time All American at Texas Tech; the number one draft choice of the Houston Oilers and Green Bay Packers; played in the Pro Bowl in 1968; played in the first and second Superbowl Playoffs with Coach Vincent T. Lombardi's Green Bay Packers; and he is the current chairman of the National Football League Alumni which represents thirty-three chapters across America.

Donny has two children, both teenagers at this writing, which partly explains his interest in and commitment to writing *Winners for Life*. He has devoted twenty-three years of his life having a wonderful time teaching and coaching youngsters. Among those who have benefited from Donny's efforts are the Special Olympics, Boys and Girls Clubs, The Gatlin Brothers' Gold Tournament, The Jerry Lewis Muscular Dystrophy event, Foster Kids, Underprivileged Youth, Stars for Children Abuse Center and the Big Brothers/Big Sisters Organization.

Donny has given over 2,000 free speeches at schools all over Texas. Today Donny is a scratch golfer, currently playing in the Celebrity Golf Tour. He is an independent insurance agent as well.

LINKIE SELTZER COHN also spent many years working with youngsters. Though her three children are teenagers no longer, while they were growing up Linkie participated wherever they were — from den mother to both the Girls and Boys Scouts, public school and religious school involvement, to sponsoring her children's social groups as well.

She initiated Human Relations Commissions in the Dallas Independent School District while working with the Greater Dallas Human Relations Commission. She also served on their board.

Linkie was nominated for the prestigious Dallas Linz Award for her many volunteer contributions to the city over the years. She was chosen to serve as a judge for the city's annual Teenage Citizenship Tribute award.

Career-wise she taught in Dallas community colleges for seven years; was Executive Director of Friends of the Hebrew University; a professional dancer, then speaker, belonging to National Speakers Association. Today she owns and operates Speakers Source International, booking celebrities, professional speakers and entertainers for corporate and association meetings.

Having belonged to many professional associations through the years, currently Linkie is a member of the International Group of Agencies and Bureaus. She is listed in Who's Who of International Women, Who's Who in the Southwest and Who's Who in the World.